Emotion Charades

Pastina Perianayagi

BookLeaf
Publishing

Presentation by *BookLeaf Publishing*

Web: www.bookleafpub.com

E-mail: info@bookleafpub.com

ISBN: 9789357619509

First edition 2023

*For Aurelia Chrissen - My playful daughter
who slingshots me around the horizon to see
what is next*

ACKNOWLEDGEMENT

Embracing 'Gratitude' to Jesus Christ for blessing me with all the goodness I could ask for from this world and for choosing to deliver me at the best of families, twice. I remember with profound respect, my ancestors and grandparents for their actions and decisions make me what I am in a way. I would like to acknowledge: My father, mother and brother who totally live for me and I for them. My husband who perfectly supports and complements me by being so good at what I am not. My father-in law, mother-in-law and sister-in-law who have been the best and always a father, mother and sister to me.

Shout out to Nancy, Rafi, Chrissen, Sreeja and all other dearest friends who were also great inspirations. Thanks to our firm- Qualitty Tools and its families who are our pillars of support, my school and teachers for instilling the love for reading at a tender age. My college and the professors who never failed to appreciate and encourage. I thank my extended family, my first employer, neighbours, colleagues and well-wishers. Many thanks to all the authors whose works I am smitten with and adore each day.

Special mention to my brother, Prince Jebaraj for his beautiful cover art and my husband, Pari Thusnavis for fixing the title to be a little more captivating!

I remember and honor the memory of our beloved Raja Mama and Arul Periappa whom we lost recently and whose care and guidance we terribly miss.

I conclude by thanking the universe in conspiring me to keep trying to be a moderate writer rather than a bad dancer or a terrible singer as I would have tried them all if this did not happen. Thank you, universe!

PREFACE

"Fiction is too beautiful to be about just one thing. It should be about everything" — Arundhati Roy

Every book, movie, incident, conversation and feeling would leave impressions in our mind that get collected like water in catchments over time and gush forth when the sluice gates of creativity open. 'Emotion Charades' is one such gentle expression through poetry - my most comfortable and favourite type of writing.

The writing process for these twenty-one poems in itself is a very rewarding experience that I am bound to cherish longer in my life. When I began writing as part of 'TheWriteAngle' writing challenge, I was hoping to seek out for references in the realms of previous published works, of timeless stories and much acclaimed reflective essays. But I ended up looking inside me: sometimes from my memories, from characters living near me, sometimes from my fears, disappointments and never fulfilled desires which was truly soul searching.

I have always felt that poetry is an aesthetic arrangement of thoughts and words which emphasize the poet's ideas but completes their implication only when complemented with the readers contemplation. It is a two-way communication. These twenty-one poems in your hand - not arranged on any order, could convince, dissuade or resonate an idea for you or could ignite a totally different one from your own personal archives. Either ways, the conclusion and its impact are with you, in your minds and should be very rewarding too, I hope. Hence, with a note of heartfelt thanks for your readership I take leave; inviting you to explore, be one with, appraise and censure this first attempt of mine which is extra special as the first happens only once.

Awe

A canopy of twinkling lights
Looking beneath us for zillion years
An embellished fabric of sparkles
Interposed by bigger luminous studs
You proudly flaunt a light show
At the centre a valiant Pole star
The interlocked constellations of zodiacs
Where nature playfully joined the dots
Sprinkled by a little cosmic dust
A spectacle to the eye

But every thirtieth day I cheat on all of you
With another celestial beauty
I fall as deep as the craters into her endless vanity
The waxing after the waning adds daily to the belle
Her beams the charmer of an enchantress
Defiling your grandeur to just a backdrop - what do I say?
I am just a poor human and she keeps coming my way
Every time I lie back and gaze
I drown in your dazzling glory
But on full moon nights I beg your mercy
She is the goddess always.

Exuberance

She walks faster than us
Wakes up alarm clocks
Never leans on any machine
Never asks anyone to assist in chores

She sweats it out when angry
She sweats it out when sad
Her days and ways are consistent
She walks faster than us.

She self-taught herself to write a new language
Spends time for others if that would at the least salvage
On days one gets tempted to just sit and gossip
She isolates and prays for everyone in worship

A human collection of motivation videos
Though she herself has watched none
My friends always want a chat with her
Just to recharge positivity by a tonne

She is always e-spirited
Yet overreacting for a joke
Sometimes she is so naïve
Trusting forward messages to the core

Always there for a pep talk.
To fiercely support, blindly love
And also, gracefully detach when it feels right
This exuberant monster whom we call mother
And yes, she always walks faster than us!

Romance

3

Our terrace moon as you like it
Shining in evanescence even throughout the day

The beautiful garden you tended to
Soaked in yesterday's showers
To an alluring green shade

Like the mint chutney you always make
To announce peace after our usual fray
I remember all about us still
Without your reminder notes in my lunch bag every day

Our dusty wedding picture on the wall
The eyes of our grand-daughter in a video call
Cold evenings when you wrap the Pashmina shawl
Keeps reminding me of it all

Our sons want me in the other hemisphere
Away from our horizon, far from our shore
How do I tell them?
That I need all of it here

Your thoughts don't make me fret or fume
And don't even make the evenings gloom
They make me young, alive and wanted for
Not memories of a love that leaves a moist eye
But memories of a romance that always left back a smile.

Anger

About a personal bouncer
A boxer, guard or watchdog
Like the row of little pawns beginning the contrivance
A tiny almond shaped line of defence

Well, him and his pair technically
Occupy hardly a few centimetres of our brain
Yet they have a hotline or so I believe
Rerouting emotions and DJing memories to relive

They have a leash on your anger
They harness it safely away
But unchain at the site of conflict
Whether you have or not a say

They know what to say to harm
And know which weapon to arm
They only know a fight or flight
But never care of the following plight

They are so much fond of a hijack
So, it is righteous to design a fallback
Take a deep breath so that they sleep away
And then tune in your rationales to begin play

AMYGDALA - a notorious element of evolution
For protection when complications had begun
But an armed mind needs to be responsible
Because anger is an unlicensed gun.

Sympathy

A chorus of alarms beeping
Both breaths laden with the antiseptic fragrance
All vitals failing sharply
Every factor for life shutting down

"Monitor and Sedate" the same old orders
To the single nurse attending both beds
The two old hospital mates now departing
A final journey to their loved ones

Countdown of pulse begins slowly
For a race to leave this unworthy world
Sucked their entire life of love
Left them bereft now

Drooping heads couldn't turn to the other
Two thankful looks at the dejected nurse
And there she held the "Hand of God"!
The ingeniously named warm latex glove

The contest to death halted now with thoughts
Tears welled both of their last prayers
"Oh, he should go first" - a dying wish
I will hold on to grieve him momentarily

I will give him love and empathy
And my last gasp of warmth to comfort
"Let me be the last one left with the glove
Punished by science's sympathy "

Triumph

Our face pressed down with boot stamps
Our respect milled
Our back embossed with flogging scars
A century old plead
For justice and equality
They scorned

Our blood shed in rebel
Our comrades massacred
Our uprisings avenged
Families sacrificed
Yet orphans thrived
They feared

Our voices empowered
Our offspring excelled
We earned
What we yearned for
We snatched
What was rightfully ours
They surrendered
A triumph!

Horror

A robed and veiled black epiphany
With pale, parched and shrunk skin
Eyes as kohled with a pointed chin
Singing under my bed curved in
On my couch or garden swing
Or always hanging around amongst my kin
Will my reflection sport an evil grin?
These are hauntings triggering adrenaline
I usually imagine and in tiptoes run back in.

This dearest friend of mine
And our noisy school girls' gang of nine
Her movie narrations are usual things
But one about a video and the evil that it brings
Her vivid descriptions chilling our spine
Huddling closer our fingers intertwined
The unique feeling that today brings smile
Back then a concerned fever for a while

Watching the movie or sequels of 'The Ring'
Every time those childhood memories spring
Her eerie modulation that petrified us listening
And the nights we woke up with rapid breathing
There was never a water well, we went close peeping
And was dreaded of the TV for many evenings
Among a hundred things fancy and glistening
Bonding us then adolescent beings
The horror stories were really frightening
And the ghosts of the past still lurking.

Happiness

The brighter stars
Nudging the lesser bright ones
To look at you together in envy

The moon beams reflecting
At your brilliant face
An inadequate match to your beauty

Your pink face pressed onto my bosom
A cute sleep-smile relishing your dream
A tiny human bringing blessings in bounty

A tangent of mischiefs and small mutiny
Cutting the waves of silence and monotony
A pair of sparkly laughing eyes
Always drying up mine when cloudy

The love that literally beckons with open arms
Only expecting mine and nothing more in returns
The angel mending scores of broken hearts
With charms laden smiles of serenity

Me the clingy creeper on the newly sprouted you
While you figure out your ways without me
Here I am wondering what would I do without you
I will fortify this treasure for eternity

Not all pains are rewarding
Not all struggles are cherished
Yet a mother loves to do it all over again
Because she gives birth to happiness.

Sorrow

His life insurance policy pre-matured
The remaining shaving cream wasted
TV commercials won over a wedding promise
Emulsion paints and economic cars lasted longer
His broken 'forever' lay cold in a coffin

A hundred people witnessed their marriage
The same hundred in the same church
To see her now married to sticky tears,
Moist cheeks and dry eyes
He had returned the wedding ring.

She grieved his unlived years
His unfulfilled wishes, his unsung laurels,
She grieved all the happy moments that she would miss
She grieved all the moments she wished to be left alone
Now wanting a refund of at least those few

Yesterday she wondered if he bothered
On the many wishes and wants she had
Today she longed for one last chance to bother him
To breathe in his soul, come out of the casket
And call out her name once more.

Dodge

A veneration not just respect
I have on you each day
I work hours for your arrival
Meticulous and aggressive would say
Yet when the others hold you in their hands
I struggle so much in a way
To bury the sharp jealousy's fang
And muffle the clamor of a heart break
I always go unnoticed
Like 'Gravity' in earth which has never failed in a day
But a movie in its name to describe 'Space'
Where it had not worked any day
One day I believe you would bump my way
Pleading for forgiveness for being so late
Oh, you and your knack of slipping away
Will not go unpunished that day
Let's see when my offerings of hard-work
Draws your sniff to my bray
Would you etch 'SUCCESS' on my breast plate
Or call it all on luck and dodge away.

Disgust

Wake up dear sister
This world is not ours today
The flowers don't bloom for us
The namings are a hoax

Your soft body abraded
Lying semi-nude in pain
Wake up soon and leave
Behold they are to come

If there is still life inside
Walk faster or if possible, run
Gathering all the pieces
Of the tatters lying besides

If they happen to see you
They will measure the ripped away skirts
Your tear smudged makeup
Will write pages of your misconduct

If you happen to reach home
And it is still open for you
Rush and lock it inside
Close your eyes and ears

A day will surely come
When patriarchy dunks itself in shame
Every wound and scar will heal
As the gibbets bear their names

Come out on a day of just
When this sinful world drowns in disgust
A new breathing world to rule
And to safely escort you to school.

Surprise

Ten thousand miles in an aluminum tube
After several sleep episodes -
Abrupt with neck pain
Landing on the city gasping
Did not end my journey

Driving another six hundred
With this good-hearted chauffeur
Who keeps honking to a minimum
So that I get some sleep

I dream of your big blue bag
Which was actually a disguise
For a box with a satin bow
And the endless chasm of gifts inside

The yummy sweets arranged on top
Of small toys for the jealous one
I pass it on to him with a stare
Eager to get to the bottom

Beautiful dresses for my short self
And beautiful clips for my long hair
The list goes on and on with
Everything I have always wanted for

Like the bag kept aside after emptying the gifts
Our lives pushed you to the side line
But this time here I come
For your platinum birthday - I don't exactly know

How old are you grandma?
What color do you like?
What is your favorite book?
What gift shall I buy?
I could never think of anything
Until I reached your home

You let out a squeal of joy
Dropping things down
Like you have just won a lottery
A happy gush in your eyes

After shamelessly filling my tummy
With your tasty food
I lie down on your lap
Like years ago, we would

I could not think of any
To surprise you grandma
What do you want from me?
I ask as naively as I could

You wanted nothing anymore
But would rather die for moments like these
A tear from my eye for doing the right thing
For I am the one with a satin bow
And my plane probably the blue bag

Confusion

With one eye open
She looked at the alarm
And jolted up on bed
As ghastly as she could

While he never dozed
His buzzing family around
Haphazard noises in the busy house
Him being the only one out of a job

A thousand voices jamming up her mind
Like a busy road where sergeants were none
" Is it right? Will it work?
Did they seem cordial? Is he the one? "

Mother coming inside his room
Stroking his forehead with all smiles
And giving him a little sweet curd
Feels like an exam day it seems weird

She liked the jewels, the beautiful clothes
So sure, of her look and pose
Unsure of everything else
And the confusion getting worse

Oh, there they are! All of his phone contacts
Not arranged alphabetically; all smiling at him here
Greeting him and patting on his back
Feels good for a moment but then nothing works

Why are flowers weighing a tonne?
Is it just a garland or a chain of iron?
Her dad who feared even her vaccine shots
Looks so accomplished while her emotions are
falling apart

The traffic jams seem comforting
Delays to the venue appealing
Suddenly the world follows him behind
And in is his private moment they collectively mind

The most decisive moment for families
Could be fixing an arranged marriage
What the bride and groom would not talk about
Are prior confusions that took them in bondage.

Envy

An abrasive metal sounding alarm
An old tape singing hymns at the neighbors
Street cries, clanking, chirping
Topping it all my mother's yelling
Versus the boring Instagram scrolls in the
restroom every morning

My best friend I wrote to in my entire diary
The red satin bands we exchanged on Friendship day
A bakery over-hearing our horror stories
The slam books that shout out aloud "Friends forever"
Versus an empty group chat with the last message
of "Happy New Year"

My earnest chats with brother about new movie
mentions
Luring my dad's attention with our own promotion
Imploring mother to join this occasion
Finally enjoying with non-caramelized popcorn at
the intermission
Versus a watch party in Netflix now that I slept
through for no reason

A time when life thrived with everything in paltry
A time now with plenty yet we just lookback and envy.

Laughter

"Ninety days" said Ford as he lazily woke up
Rubbing his eyes and trying hard to spark up
Thoughts of D-day and the incident that led to the break up
With his third girl Fanny. And all his trials to bridge up
The small crack had only in vain always brought up
Great crevices in the relation. And finally locking up
In his closet he thinks of soon catching up
With some dear friends and arrange for a formal patch-up
With a lot of plans, dress up and ketch-up
His friend Jack drives to her place to pick her up
The moron driver misses her house in a mix up
Poor Ford calls on to ask her was-sup?
She does not mind a public transport and finally makes up
To the spot where the house party is planned for the
patch-up
Welcoming her in through the door he looks up
And spots a serious flaw in the planned build up
Of a "SORRY" board in the doorway carefully hung up
But carelessly nailed by Jim to hit the passer bye without a
heads-up
Apologizing and tending to her bruised forehead they get
seated up
In a specially set dinner table for a cozy sup
After playing 'Don Perry' and filling their glasses up
He remembers the duck roast that is in the oven and locked
up
Quite a few long hours it has been cooked up
By his sweet friend John who only forgot to fetch it up
Until the moment when a smoky air catches up
And Fanny's flared nostrils and her chin pointed up
She cools down after some time and finally looks up

To forgive him for all the follies, blunders and mess-up
Finally, at the most awaited moment of holy smooch up
The door-bell rings and Ford gets started up
For the stupid driver Jack had brought the wrong girl to the
set up
She was the girl before Fanny whom Ford used to cuddle
up
Jack had faithfully convinced her during the ride to bring
her moods up
That she rushes to Ford in a second and throws her arms up
An immediate apocalypse of events follows up
Fanny rushes out of the house Followed by Ford with his
hands up
On his cheek to hide the pink finger patches that clearly
showed up
Sorrowfully rushing up he glimpsed at his three friends
who stood up
At a distance partying and greeting him with their thumbs
up!
For poor fellows they thought that it was a successful
PATCH-UP!

Nostalgia

A string of spilled black pearls
On tattered brown pages
Delicately turning grandma's handwritten recipes
A taste that lingers through ages

An ancient gramophone collecting dust
Sitting on an old vinyl record
A veiled woman at the fore of a minaret
"Pakeezah"read the words in bold

Ceramic pickle jars she can no longer carry
Now sooty and sticky to touch
Raw mangoes soaked in them every summer
My memories still soaking there too

Grandpa's thick bounded book on Nature
A Reader's Digest special copy
His lesson to a three-year-old me on blood sucking
insects
"Lice, leech, mosquito & bug" - They still infest my
memory

Their home once a cozy cottage
For my fairy land of imaginations
It seems aged now to a perfect time machine
Taking me to the land of personal nostalgia

Fear

Those yellow eyes
Behind the dim bushes
The howls that follow
And cease on turning back
The masked stares and sharp knives
A groping hand or just a shadow?
Accidents and derails at every quest
Tempests and earthquakes
At the Almighty's behest
Bankruptcy and theft of the little we own
Trolls and embarrassments
From those who scorn
Stings, bites and poisons at the wild unknown
Sickness and surgeries
By a typo in genetic code
Palsy and death of the dearly beloved
And a thousand more dangers for the dreaded
Fear is a necessary premonition
Which in overdose becomes a dysfunction
And the farthest distance we trod to cross our fears
Is sometimes only the length of our minds.

Anxiety

One day almost my entire nation
    Stood frozen but impatiently
While traffic seemed, grid locked
    Yet the sergeants cared less unusually

Old aged hypertensives
    Living cautiously in emotional equilibrium
Jolted emotions through highs and lows
    Watching a televised medium

Devoted mothers and housewives
    Locked up in prayers at their sanctuary
Never mentioned families and kids
    In their chants that day on the contrary

Little children sent to play
    On the streets were forgotten
Nothing valuable was precious for the time
    Yet nothing seemed stolen

We all worshipped superstition
    Remaining frozen every moment
Poor many holding back their pee
    Avoid any unlucky big movement

One and the same prayer
    Every religion could witness
Every stranger a fellow brother
    Who held our hands to ease tenseness

We demonstrated patriotism
    To the whole world in an evening
Our hearts cried "Vande Mataram"
    Cheering up every ball in that last inning

Our beloved savior M.S.Dhoni -
    The greatest of captains on guard
 Owning a doctorate of winning in style
    Every match that was outright hard

Yet the nation was fearful and stressed
    Until we heard the triumphant fireworks
Breaking the rhythm of rapid heart-beats
    With exultant whoops, went berserk

Why is this final match of a cricket world cup?
    A nail-biting phenomenon
Why did it become a roller-coaster ride?
    Through nervous and restless apprehension

An unfulfilled yearning
  The dream of this country
Not just a five-hour journey from anxiety to
achievement
Truly a lifetime experience in history.

Calm

Multiple snoozed alarms turn the day on
To a life that teaches us not to care
Even if someone stole the sun

Seventy notifications flash and appear
In a phone that continuously rings
Just pretending to be useful until we hit Clear

Hunting wealth like programmed cyborgs
To snatch, kill or die but not think
Yet lock the heap up in life's brittle coffers

Every day is a storm carrying us like junk
Spinning at thousand miles around
Until we fall down and perish unsung

If by chance one day we pause
Without a pandemic, war or any pressing cause
And reach the eye where the storm calms

Where world unwinds on life's couch
A poise silver line of nature and science
And plenty of time for their healing touch

What we need today is a calm
A content half stop to this vicious cycle
A tiny prick in our hamster ball.

Disappointment

Seven children at equal intervals
Every child fed and provided
A basic facility to educate
But a lot of space to ideate
An income that does not steeplechase
Nobody to sit around and appraise
Contentment their biggest wealth
Happiness in just a meagre of abundance

A small yet comfy cottage
At the foot of a sandy beach
Fresh fish for daily feast
Palm toddy for evening chill outs
Backyard gifts of sweet coconuts
Heaps of fallen fruits with cashew-nuts
No, I am not talking about a vacation in Hawaii
This was the staple of the whole village life

Nutritious, organic, chemical free
Not mere fancy labels but reality
Never heard of diabetes or daily pills
No fitness tracker and treadmills
Creativity not bound by vendition
Gentler footprints of carbon
Rest with sunset and
Toil with sunrise
A simple yet meaningful mantra of life

Just as how we awe at age old stars
We do envy the peaceful life of our ancestors
Though crowned with pride of techs
And clothed with extravagant modern science
We do go all coy and also occasionally sigh
Disappointed of our life's quality versus their highs.

Hunger

Thirteen days she counted
On a silent commute to home
The cool breeze closed her puffy eyes
A new world sans her mother

An unwelcoming empty gateway
No more traditional Kolam
At the fore of a cold and empty house
In the place of her once happy home

A lot of happenings to share
Yet nobody anymore would care
The hot ginger tea she slurped while narrating
Munching mom's homemade savories went missing

An unfamiliar grumble in her tummy
A craving for something yummy
She forayed to forage the kitchen
Then the fridge - the leftover's dominion

'Empty vessels make the most noise'
Every vessel seemed empty in the house
Yet her stomach was the noisiest she thought
Her hunger had sustained, the search could not

All ingredients were there but no food
Like a world full of mothers but not hers
Had only mother known this was the end
She would have cooked and hidden something
To last every day until the world's end.

This unknown monster her mother guarded against
Seemed rumbling strongly every minute now
She totally broke down crying, helpless
And hungry for her mother's love.

www.ingramcontent.com/pod-product-compliance
Lightning Source LLC
La Vergne TN
LVHW010934200726

843509LV00013B/2212